PLANT-BASED CA

COOKBOOK FOR BEGINNERS

"Flavorful Plant-Based Cardiac Diet
Recipes for Beginners"

Allie Nagel

Copyright © 2023 by Allie Nagel

INTRODUCTION

"I hate this feeling," thought Louise as she walked slowly up the stairs, gasping for air and aching all over. She had recently been diagnosed with cardiac issues, and her life had become an endless series of struggles.

At first, she barely noticed the onset of the symptoms, but the constant chest pain and difficulty breathing forced her to see a doctor. It was then that she found out to her horror that she had severe cardiac problems.

Her doctors had put her on a strict regimen, limiting her activity, advising her to avoid certain foods, and recommending medications to regulate her blood pressure and keep her condition manageable.

At first, Louise was terrified and unable to accept the idea of the changes she needed to make to her life. She believed that her life was over and that she was doomed to spend the rest of her days confined to her bed.

But one day she heard about some success stories of people with similar conditions. With renewed hope, she decided to take matters into her own hands and try to improve her health herself.

So, Louise began to do her research. She researched holistic methods of healing and changed her diet to exclude unhealthy foods and to include nutrient-rich fruits and vegetables.

She started an exercise program tailored for her individual needs and was soon able to slowly add more activities to her routine. She also looked for ways to reduce stress levels in her life and focused on positive thinking.

Amazingly, with time, Louise started to notice a real improvement in her condition, and the symptoms started to diminish. She was able to gradually increase her activity levels and even started going out to meet friends and family more often. She felt like a different person.

In time, Louise was able to reclaim her life and enjoy the activities she had been forced to abandon because of her cardiac condition.

CHAPTER 1

An Overview on Plant Based Cardiac Diet for Beginners

The Plant-based Cardiac Diet is a lifestyle approach for managing heart disease.

It is a low-fat, Plant-based whole foods diet with the goal of reducing cholesterol, improving blood pressure, and reducing the risk of heart attack and stroke.

Its main focus is on eating Plant-based whole foods like fruits, vegetables, legumes, and nuts and seeds instead of animal-based products like meat, cheese, and eggs.

This diet has been adopted by healthcare providers and heart health organizations as an effective way to prevent and treat heart conditions.

Studies have found that eating a Plant-based diet may reduce cholesterol levels, lower blood pressure, and reduce the risk of coronary artery disease and other cardiovascular events.

For beginners, it's important to start slow and be consistent. Start by incorporating more fruits and vegetables into your diet and limiting your consumption of animal-based products. This means avoiding high fat meats, processed meats, and added sugars.

Instead, focus on choosing a variety of nutrient-dense Plant-based foods such as legumes, nuts and seeds, whole grains, and fruits and vegetables.

In addition to food choices, physical activity is also an important part of the Plant-based cardiac diet.

The American Heart Association recommends at least 150 minutes of moderate intensity aerobic exercise per week.

This might include walking, jogging, swimming, or cycling. Strength and flexibility training can also help improve overall health.

Finally, it's important to track your progress. Keeping a daily food and exercise journal can help you stay on track and make necessary adjustments if needed.

DISCLAIMER

This cookbook is intended to provide general information and recipes. The recipes provided in this cookbook are not intended to replace or be a substitute for medical advice from a physician.

The reader should consult a healthcare professional for any specific medical advice, diagnosis or treatment.

Any specific dietary advice provided in this cookbook is not intended to replace or be a substitute for medical advice from a physician.

The author is not responsible or liable for any adverse effects experienced by readers of this cookbook as a result of following the recipes or dietary advice provided.

The author makes no representations or warranties of any kind (express or implied) as to the accuracy, completeness, reliability or suitability of the recipes provided in this cookbook.

The author disclaims any and all liability for any damages arising out of the use or misuse of the recipes provided in this cookbook. The reader must also take care to ensure that the recipes provided in this cookbook are prepared and cooked safely.

The recipes provided in this cookbook are for informational purposes only and should not be used as a substitute for professional medical advice, diagnosis or treatment.

TABLE OF CONTENTS

10 Benefits of a Plant Based Cardiac Diet for Beginners

1. Reduced LDL Cholesterol: A plant based diet is naturally low in saturated fat and cholesterol, which can help reduce your levels of LDL cholesterol ("bad" cholesterol).

2. Boosted Antioxidants: Eating a Plant-based diet also increases your antioxidant intake, which helps fight inflammation, which is a major risk factor for heart disease.

3. Improved Blood Pressure and Triglycerides: Research shows that eating a diet rich in plant foods can help improve blood pressure and triglyceride levels, both of which are risk factors for cardiovascular disease.

4. Increased Fiber Intake: Plant foods are rich in fiber, which helps slow the absorption of sugar in your diet and can help lower your risk of heart disease.

5. Lower Risk of Diabetes: Eating a Plant-based diet can help keep your blood sugar levels steady, which reduces your risk of developing type 2 diabetes.

6. Reduced Risk of Obesity: Eating a Plant-based diet helps promote a healthy body weight, which can reduce your risk of obesity and its associated complications, such as heart disease.

7. Reduced Risk of Cancer: Research has linked a Plant-based diet to a reduced risk of certain types of cancer, such as colon cancer.

8. Improved Bone Health: Eating a Plant-based diet can help improve bone health, as it contains plenty of calcium, magnesium, and other nutrients important for healthy bones.

9. Reduced Inflammation: Plant-based diets are naturally anti-inflammatory, as they contain vitamins and minerals that work to reduce inflammation in the body.

10. Improved Heart Health: Eating a Plant-based diet can help reduce your risk of heart disease, by reducing cholesterol, improving blood pressure, and more.

CHAPTER 2

14-Day Meal Plan

DAY 1

Breakfast: Spanish Omelette with Sweet Potato

Lunch: Veggie Crackers & Almond Butter

Dinner: Kale and Brown Rice Casserole

DAY 2

Breakfast: Baked Sweet Potato with Cashew Cream

Lunch: Couscous Salad with Greens and Herbs

Dinner: Vegetable StirFry with WholeGrain Rice

DAY 3

Breakfast: Nut and Seed Oatmeal Bars

Lunch: Lentil & Chickpea Stew

Dinner: Baked Spaghetti Squash with White Beans and Arugula

DAY 4

Breakfast: Mung Bean Pancakes

Lunch: Avocado & Quinoa Wrap

Dinner: Chickpea and Spinach Curry

DAY 5

Breakfast: Banana Date Smoothie

Lunch: Baked Sweet Potato with Black Bean Salsa

Dinner: Quinoa Veggie Burgers

DAY 6

Breakfast: Chia Seed Pudding

Lunch: Roasted Veggie & Hummus Wrap

Dinner: Vegetable StirFry with WholeGrain Rice

DAY 7

Breakfast: Overnight Oats with Berries

Lunch: Chickpea & Kale Salad

6. Place in oven and bake for about 25 minutes or until the omelette is golden brown and cooked through.

7. Remove from oven and season with salt and pepper as desired. Sprinkle with cilantro and serve warm.

Serving Suggestion: Serve with a side salad

Baked Sweet Potato with Cashew Cream

Enjoy this vegan-friendly and energy-packed meal that is high in fiber, magnesium and potassium. Ideal for those suffering from cardiac disease.

Ingredients:

2 medium sweet potatoes

2 tablespoons olive oil

1/2 teaspoon garlic powder

1/4 teaspoon salt

1/4 cup raw cashew Cream

2 tablespoons maple syrup

1 teaspoon smoked paprika

Chopped chives for garnish

Preparation Time: 30 minutes

Method of Preparation:

1. Preheat oven to 375°F (190°C).

2. Line a baking sheet with parchment paper.

3. Place the sweet potatoes on the prepared baking sheet and brush with the olive oil. Sprinkle with garlic powder and salt.

4. Transfer to oven and bake for about 25 minutes or until the sweet potatoes are tender and slightly golden brown.

5. Meanwhile, in a small bowl, combine the cashew cream, maple syrup, and smoked paprika and mix together.

6. Once the sweet potatoes are baked, transfer to a plate. Drizzle with the cashew cream and garnish with chives, if desired.

Serving Suggestion: Serve with a side of fresh fruits or steamed vegetables.

Nut and Seed Oatmeal Bars

Treat yourself to these healthy bars that are packed with fiber and low in saturated fat, ideal for anyone with a cardiac disease.

Ingredients:

1 cup rolled oats

½ cup shredded coconut

½ cup pumpkin seeds

¼ cup almond flour

¼ cup chia seeds

¼ cup hemp seeds

¼ cup flax meal

¼ teaspoon cinnamon

½ cup rice malt syrup

½ cup nut butter

2 tablespoons coconut oil

Preparation Time: 45 minutes

Method of Preparation:

1. Preheat oven to 350F.

2. Line a square baking dish with parchment paper.

3. In a large bowl, combine the oats, shredded coconut, pumpkin seeds, almond flour, chia seeds, hemp seeds, flax meal, and cinnamon.

4. In a small saucepan, combine the rice malt syrup, nut butter, and coconut oil and heat over low heat until fully combined.

5. Pour the wet ingredients over the dry ingredients and mix until evenly combined.

6. Transfer the mixture to the prepared baking dish and press down evenly.

7. Place in oven and bake for 20-25 minutes or until the bars are golden brown.

8. Remove from oven and cool completely before cutting into bars.

Serving Suggestion: Serve as a snack or for breakfast with a dollop of Greek yogurt or almond milk.

Mung Bean Pancakes

Easy to make and filled with fiber, magnesium, phosphorus, and potassium, these mung bean pancakes are great for those suffering from cardiac disease looking to eat a healthy meal.

Ingredients:

1 cup mung beans, soaked for 6 hours

2 tablespoons nutritional yeast

1 teaspoon cumin

1 teaspoon garlic powder

1/2 teaspoon sea salt

1/2 teaspoon ground pepper

2 tablespoons olive oil

1/4 cup water

Preparation Time: 30 minutes

Method of Preparation:

1. Drain and rinse the mung beans, then place in a blender or food processor with the remaining ingredients.

2. Blend or process until a smooth paste forms.

3. Heat a skillet over medium heat and add the olive oil.

4. When the oil is hot, add the mung bean mixture to the skillet in 45 small pancakes.

5. Cook for 35 minutes, until golden brown and crispy, then flip and cook for another 35 minutes.

Serving Suggestion: Serve with some salsa, avocado, or vegan cream cheese for a delicious breakfast.

Banana Date Smoothie

Enjoy this creamy and delicious smoothie, made with creamy banana, dates, and non-dairy milk. Ideal for anyone with cardiac disease due to its good source of potassium.

Ingredients:

1 frozen banana

1/2 cup unsweetened Plant-based milk

2 Medjool dates, pitted

1 teaspoon almond butter

1 teaspoon chia seeds

1/4 teaspoon ground cinnamon

1 tablespoon nut butter

Preparation Time: 10 minutes

Method of Preparation:

1. Place the banana in a high-speed blender and process until broken down.

2. Add the milk, dates, almond butter, chia seeds, and cinnamon and blend until smooth.

3. Taste and adjust flavor as desired, adding more dates for sweetness if necessary.

4. Add ice cubes if desired and blend until smooth.

5. Pour the smoothie into a glass and top with nut butter.

Serving Suggestion: Serve with a side of fresh fruits for a nutritious breakfast.

Chia Seed Pudding

Create this light and creamy pudding, made with chia seeds that are full of omega3 fatty acids and fiber. Perfect for those with cardiac disease with its low saturated fat content.

Ingredients:

1/2 cup chia seeds

2 cups unsweetened Plant-based milk

2 teaspoons pure vanilla extract

2 tablespoons maple syrup

Toppings of choice (fruit, nuts, seeds, coconut flakes, etc.)

Preparation Time: 10 minutes (including soaking time)

Method of Preparation:

1. In a medium bowl, combine the chia seeds, milk, vanilla extract, and maple syrup.

2. Stir well to combine and let sit for at least 1 hour or until the chia seeds have expanded and a pudding-like consistency is achieved.

3. Taste and adjust flavor as desired.

4. Divide the pudding among 4 small bowls or glasses and top with desired toppings.

Serving Suggestion: This pudding is delicious served with fresh fruit, nuts, or seeds.

Overnight Oats with Berries

Achieve this easy and hearty breakfast each morning with oats, berries, and nuts. Full of vitamins, minerals, and fiber, this breakfast is great for someone with cardiac disease.

Ingredients:

1/2 cup rolled oats

1 cup unsweetened Plant-based milk

2 tablespoons chia seeds

1/2 teaspoon pure vanilla extract

1/4 teaspoon ground cinnamon

1/2 cup mixed fresh berries

2 tablespoons maple syrup

Preparation Time: 10 minutes (including overnight soaking time)

Method of Preparation:

1. Place the oats in a bowl and pour the milk over them.

2. Stir in the chia seeds, vanilla extract, and cinnamon.

3. Cover the bowl and refrigerate overnight.

4. In the morning, stir in the fresh berries and maple syrup.

5. Divide the oats among 2 small bowls or glasses and top with more fresh berries, if desired.

Serving Suggestion: Enjoy this savory/sweet oatmeal with a side of nut butter or a dollop of Greek yogurt.

Hummus Avocado Toast

Indulge in this fiber-filled and Plant-based meal with hummus and avocado. Ideal for anyone with cardiac disease due to its healthy and heart-healthy fats.

Ingredients:

2 slices sprouted wheat bread

1/4 cup hummus

1/2 ripe avocado, sliced

Sprouts or micro-greens

Hot sauce or paprika, for garnish

Preparation Time: 10 minutes

Method of Preparation:

1. Toast the sprouted wheat bread.

2. Spread the hummus on the toast.

3. Top with slices of avocado and sprouts or micro-greens.

4. Drizzle with hot sauce or sprinkle with paprika for flavor, if desired.

Serving Suggestion: Serve this toast as a light lunch or snack with fresh fruits or vegetables.

Quinoa Porridge

Start your day right with this quinoa porridge, packed with fiber and protein. Great for anyone with cardiac disease looking for an energizing breakfast that is easy to digest.

Ingredients:

1/2 cup quinoa, rinsed

1 cup unsweetened Plant-based milk

1 teaspoon ground cinnamon

2 tablespoons maple syrup

1/2 cup fresh fruit

1/4 cup nuts or seeds

Preparation Time: 15 minutes

Method of Preparation:

1. Place the quinoa in a medium saucepan with the milk, cinnamon, and maple syrup.

2. Bring to a boil over medium-high heat, then reduce heat and simmer for about 10 minutes or until the quinoa is soft and most of the liquid is absorbed.

3. Remove from heat and let cool for a few minutes.

4. Transfer the quinoa to a bowl and top with fresh fruit, nuts or seeds, and a dollop of nut butter.

Serving Suggestion: Serve as a breakfast or snack with Greek yogurt or nut milk.

Sprouted Wheat Toast with Nut Butter

Satisfy your cravings with this tasty and filling toast, high in healthy fats and fiber. Perfect for those with cardiac disease looking for a healthy breakfast.

Ingredients:

2 slices sprouted wheat bread

2 tablespoons nut butter

Honey or maple syrup, for garnish

Preparation Time: 5 minutes

Method of Preparation:

1. Toast the sprouted wheat bread.

2. Spread the nut butter on the toast.

3. Drizzle with honey or maple syrup and enjoy.

Serving Suggestion: Serve with a side of fresh fruit or a glass of Plant-based milk for a delicious, healthy breakfast.

LUNCH

Veggie Crackers & Almond Butter

This crunchy snack provides a nutritious and tasty source of dietary fiber, protein, and healthy fats, beneficial for those with cardiac disease.

Ingredients:

1 cup wholewheat crackers

1/4 cup almond butter

Optional garnish: sunflower, pumpkin, or hemp seeds

Preparation Time: 10 minutes

Method of Preparation:

1. Preheat the oven to 350°F.

2. Place the crackers onto a baking sheet.

3. Bake in the preheated oven for 8-10 minutes, until lightly golden brown.

4. Remove from the oven and let cool.

5. Drizzle the almond butter over the cooled crackers and sprinkle with the desired amount of sunflower, pumpkin, or hemp seeds.

Serving Suggestion: Serve with a side of fresh fruit.

Couscous Salad with Greens and Herbs

A delicious light meal, this salad contains vital nutrients for those suffering with cardiac disease such as magnesium, iron, and vitamins A, C and K.

Ingredients:

1 cup couscous

2 cups vegetable stock

2 cups fresh spinach or arugula

1/2 cup grape tomatoes, halved

1/2 cup chopped celery

1/4 cup sliced green onions

2 tablespoons olive oil

2 tablespoons freshly chopped herbs (e.g. parsley, basil, dill)

Juice of 1/2 lemon

Salt and pepper to taste

Preparation Time: 30 minutes

Method of Preparation:

1. In a medium pot, bring the stock to a boil.

2. Once boiling, add the couscous, stirring until combined.

3. Reduce the heat to low and cover the pot with a lid.

4. Cook for 12-15 minutes, stirring occasionally.

5. Once the couscous is cooked, remove it from the heat and transfer to a large bowl.

6. Add the spinach, tomatoes, celery, green onions, olive oil, herbs, lemon juice, salt, and pepper.

7. Toss all the ingredients together until combined.

Serving Suggestion: Serve chilled or at room temperature.

Lentil & Chickpea Stew

This heartwarming stew is packed with protein, antioxidants, and dietary fiber, while providing low-fat, lowsodium nutrition, perfect for heart health.

Ingredients:

1 tablespoon olive oil

1 medium onion, diced

2 cloves garlic, minced

2 cups vegetable broth

1 cup cooked lentils

1 cup cooked chickpeas

1 teaspoon dried oregano

1 teaspoon ground cumin

1 teaspoon dried thyme

2 tablespoons tomato paste

Salt and pepper to taste

Preparation Time: 30 minutes

Method of Preparation:

1. Heat the oil in a large pot over medium-high heat.

2. Add the onion and garlic and cook until softened, about 5 minutes.

3. Add the vegetable broth, lentils, chickpeas, oregano, cumin, and thyme.

4. Bring the mixture to a boil, then reduce heat to low, and simmer for 20 minutes.

5. Stir in the tomato paste and season with salt and pepper.

6. Cook for 5 more minutes.

Serving Suggestion: Serve with a side of steamed vegetables or a slice of wholewheat toast.

Avocado & Quinoa Wrap

This wrap provides a satisfying meal with healthy fats,

protein, and dietary fiber, all important for those managing cardiac disease.

Ingredients:

1/2 cup cooked quinoa

1 ripe avocado, peeled and sliced

1/4 cup diced red onion

2 large wholewheat tortillas

Salt and pepper to taste

Preparation Time: 15 minutes

Method of Preparation:

1. In a medium bowl, combine the cooked quinoa, avocado, and red onion.

2. Mix until ingredients are evenly combined and season with salt and pepper.

3. Spread the mixture onto the tortillas, dividing evenly.

4. Fold up the bottom and sides of the tortillas to form a wrap.

Serving Suggestion: Serve with a side of your favorite salsa or dip.

Baked Sweet Potato with Black Bean Salsa

A flavorful mix of fiber-packed sweet potato and wholesome black beans, this nutritious dish is ideal for those with cardiac disease.

Ingredients:

2 sweet potatoes, cut into cubes

1 tablespoon olive oil

1 teaspoon ground cumin

1/2 teaspoon garlic powder

1 cup cooked black beans

1/4 cup diced red onion

1/4 cup chopped fresh cilantro

2 tablespoons lime juice

Salt and pepper to taste

Preparation Time: 45 minutes

Method of Preparation:

1. Preheat the oven to 400°F.

2. Place the sweet potatoes in a bowl and add the olive oil, cumin, garlic powder, salt, and pepper. Toss until all the potatoes are evenly coated.

3. Spread the potatoes in a single layer on a baking sheet and bake for 30-35 minutes, until golden brown and crisp.

4. In a medium bowl, combine the beans, onion, cilantro, and lime juice.

5. Once the potatoes are cooked, top each potato with the black bean salsa.

Serving Suggestion: Serve with a side of wilted greens or a green salad.

Roasted Veggie & Hummus Wrap

With vitamins, minerals, antioxidants, and fiber, this tasty wrap is a great choice for those with cardiac disease seeking flavorful nutrition.

Ingredients:

1/2 cup cubed eggplant

1/2 cup cubed zucchini

1/2 cup cubed yellow squash

1/2 cup cubed bell pepper

1 tablespoon olive oil

1 teaspoon dried oregano

1 large wholewheat tortilla

2 tablespoons hummus

Salt and pepper to taste

Preparation Time: 25 minutes

Method of Preparation:

1. Preheat the oven to 400°F.

2. Place the vegetables in a bowl and add the olive oil, oregano, salt, and pepper. Toss until all the vegetables are evenly coated.

3. Spread the vegetables in a single layer on a baking sheet and bake for 20-25 minutes, until golden brown and crisp.

4. Spread the hummus on the tortilla and top with the roasted vegetables.

5. Fold up the bottom and sides of the tortilla to form a wrap.

Serving Suggestion: Serve with a side of fresh fruits or nuts.

Chickpea & Kale Salad

Packed with essential minerals, protein, and dietary fiber, this salad provides vital nutrition for those with cardiac disease.

Ingredients:

1 cup cooked chickpeas

2 cups chopped kale

2 tablespoons olive oil

Juice of 1/2 lemon

1/4 cup chopped fresh herbs (e.g. parsley, cilantro, dill)

Salt and pepper to taste

Preparation Time: 15 minutes

Method of Preparation:

1. In a large bowl, combine the chickpeas, kale, olive oil, lemon juice, herbs, salt, and pepper.

2. Mix until ingredients are evenly combined.

Serving Suggestion: Serve over your favorite grain, such as quinoa or brown rice.

Grilled Tofu & Veggie Skewers

Protein-packed tofu and nutrient-rich veggies combined together in a delicious meal, perfect for those with cardiac problems.

Ingredients:

1 block firm tofu, cut into cubes

1 cup cubed bell peppers

1 large zucchini, cut into thick slices

1/4 red onion, cut into thick slices

1/4 cup olive oil

2 tablespoons dried oregano

2 tablespoons freshly chopped parsley

Salt and pepper to taste

Preparation Time: 25 minutes

Method of Preparation:

1. Preheat the oven's grill setting to medium-high heat.

2. Place the tofu, bell peppers, zucchini, and red onion into a large bowl.

3. Add the olive oil, oregano, parsley, salt, and pepper.

4. Toss until all the vegetables and tofu are evenly coated.

5. Thread the vegetables and tofu onto skewers.

6. Place the skewers on the preheated grill and cook for 15-20 minutes, turning occasionally, until cooked through.

Serving Suggestion: Serve with a side of brown rice or a green salad.

Edamame & Avocado Rice Bowl

This nutritious meal combines vitamins, antioxidants, and healthy fats, beneficial for those with cardiac disease.

Ingredients:

1 cup cooked brown rice

1/2 cup cooked edamame

1 ripe avocado, peeled and diced

2 tablespoons freshly chopped cilantro

Juice of 1/2 lemon

Salt and pepper to taste

Preparation Time: 10 minutes

Method of Preparation:

1. Place the cooked rice in a bowl.

2. Top with the cooked edamame, diced avocado, cilantro, lemon juice, salt, and pepper.

3. Mix until ingredients are combined.

Serving Suggestion: Serve with a side of steamed vegetables or a green salad.

Veggie & Tofu Lettuce Wraps

A light and nutritious dinner, these wraps provide a delicious source of protein, dietary fiber, and vitamins, perfect for those managing cardiac health.

Ingredients:

1 tablespoon olive oil

1/2 cup chopped onion

1/2 cup chopped mushrooms

1/2 cup diced bell peppers

1/2 cup cubed firm tofu

2 tablespoons freshly chopped herbs (e.g. parsley, basil, dill)

Salt and pepper to taste

4 large lettuce leaves

Preparation Time: 15 minutes

Method of Preparation:

1. Heat the oil in a large skillet over medium-high heat.

2. Add the onion, mushrooms, bell peppers, and tofu, stirring until the vegetables are softened and the tofu is lightly browned.

3. Add the herbs, salt, and pepper, and cook for 5 more minutes.

4. Spoon the mixture into lettuce leaves.

Serving Suggestion: Serve with a side of hummus or your favorite salsa.

DINNER

Kale and Brown Rice Casserole

Perfect for those with cardiac disease as it helps to reduce cholesterol and reduce the risk of stroke.

Ingredients:

4 cups cooked brown rice

3 cups chopped kale

2 tablespoons olive oil

1 cup diced onion

1 cup diced celery

1 cup diced carrots

2 cloves garlic, minced

2 teaspoons dried parsley

1 teaspoon dried oregano

1/2 teaspoon dried thyme

1/2 teaspoon sea salt

1/4 teaspoon ground black pepper

Preparation Time: 25 minutes

Method of Preparation:

1. Preheat oven to 375°F.

2. In a large pot over medium heat, heat olive oil, and sauté onion, celery, and carrots until softened, about 5 minutes.

3.Add garlic and sauté one minute more.

4.Stir in parsley, oregano, thyme, salt, and black pepper and turn off the heat.

5.In a large bowl, mix cooked brown rice and sautéed vegetables until well-combined.

6.Add chopped kale and stir until fully mixed.

7.Transfer to a 9x13inch baking dish and bake for 20 minutes.

Serving Suggestions: Serve with your favorite steamed vegetable or a leafy green salad.

Vegetable Stir-Fry with Whole Grain Rice Baked

An excellent source of folate, magnesium and fiber, it's beneficial for those with cardiac disease, helping to lower cholesterol.

Ingredients:

2 tablespoons olive oil

1 onion, diced

2 cloves garlic, minced

1 red bell pepper, diced

1 cup diced carrots

1 cup diced celery

2 cups broccoli florets

1 cup edamame

1/2 teaspoon sea salt

1/4 teaspoon ground black pepper

1 cup cooked wholegrain rice

2 tablespoons low-sodium tamari

2 tablespoons freshly squeezed lemon juice

Preparation Time: 25 minutes

Method of Preparation:

1. Preheat oven to 350°F.

2. Heat oil in a large skillet over medium heat.

3. Add onion, garlic, bell pepper, carrots, and celery and cook for about 5 minutes, stirring frequently.

4. Add broccoli, edamame, salt, and pepper and stir-fry for 2 minutes.

5. Remove from heat and add cooked rice, tamari, and lemon juice and stir until combined.

6. Transfer to a greased 9x13inch baking dish and bake for 20 minutes.

Serving Suggestions: Serve with your favorite steamed vegetable or a lightly dressed salad.

Spaghetti Squash with White Beans and Arugula

Low in calories and fat, its high fiber content helps reduce the risk of cardiac disease, helping to keep the heart healthy.

Ingredients:

1 medium spaghetti squash

2 tablespoons olive oil

2 cloves garlic, minced

1 (15ounce) can white beans, drained and rinsed

2 cups baby arugula

1/2 teaspoon sea salt

1/4 teaspoon ground black pepper

2 tablespoons freshly squeezed lemon juice

Preparation Time: 45 minutes

Method of Preparation:

1. Preheat oven to 400°F.

2. Slice squash in half lengthwise and scoop out seeds.

3. Place squash halves cut side up on a baking sheet, and drizzle with olive oil.

4. Roast for 30 minutes.

5. While squash is roasting, heat a large skillet over medium heat.

6. Add garlic and cook for 1 minute.

7. Add white beans, arugula, salt, and pepper and cook until heated through, about 5 minutes.

8. When squash is finished roasting, remove from oven and carefully scrape out strands with a fork.

9. Add squash strands to the skillet and toss to combine.

10. Add lemon juice and stir.

Serving Suggestions: Serve as a side dish with your favorite protein, or enjoy as a main course topped with your favorite nut cheese or nondairy yogurt.

Chickpea and Spinach Curry

This flavorful meal can help to reduce inflammation and control cholesterol levels, making it a great option for those with cardiac disease.

Ingredients:

2 tablespoons olive oil

1 onion, diced

2 cloves garlic, minced

2 teaspoons freshly grated ginger

2 teaspoons curry powder

1 teaspoon ground cumin

1/2 teaspoon ground coriander

1/2 teaspoon sea salt

1 (15ounce) can chickpeas, drained and rinsed

1 (14.5ounce) can diced tomatoes

1 cup low-sodium vegetable broth

2 cups packed baby spinach

Preparation Time: 20 minutes

Method of Preparation:

1. Heat oil in a large skillet over medium heat.

2. Add onion and cook until softened, about 5 minutes.

3. Add garlic, ginger, curry powder, cumin, coriander, and salt and cook for 1 minute more.

4. Add chickpeas, tomatoes, and vegetable broth and bring ingredients to a boil.

5. Reduce heat to low and simmer for 5 minutes.

6. Add spinach and simmer for an additional 5 minutes.

Serving Suggestions: Serve with a side of brown basmati rice or steamed quinoa.

Quinoa Veggie Burgers

This delicious veggie burger is full of nutrition and flavor, providing plenty of vitamins, minerals, and fiber. Perfect for those with cardiac disease, its Plant-based protein helps to reduce cholesterol levels.

Ingredients:

1 cup uncooked quinoa

2 cups low-sodium vegetable broth

1 cup mushrooms, diced

1/2 cup diced onion

1/2 cup diced red bell pepper

2 cloves garlic, minced

1 (15ounce) can black beans, drained and rinsed

1/3 cup panko bread crumbs

2 tablespoons nutritional yeast

2 tablespoons freshly squeezed lemon juice

1 teaspoon Italian seasoning

1/2 teaspoon sea salt

1/4 teaspoon ground black pepper

Preparation Time: 40 minutes

Method of Preparation:

1. Cook quinoa in vegetable broth according to package directions.

2. Heat a large skillet over medium heat and add mushrooms, onion, and bell pepper.

3.Cook for 5 minutes until vegetables are softened.

4.Add garlic and cook for 1 minute more.

5.Remove from heat and add black beans, cooked quinoa, panko bread crumbs, nutritional yeast, lemon juice, Italian seasoning, salt, and pepper and stir until combined.

6.Divide mixture into 8 equal portions and form into patties.

7.In the same skillet, heat extravirgin olive oil over medium heat and cook veggie burgers for 8 minutes on each side.

Serving Suggestions: Serve on a wholegrain bun with your favorite burger toppings.

Vegetable Stir-Fry with WholeGrain Rice

Fiber-rich and low in fat, it's great for those with cardiac disease since its anti-inflammatory qualities help to reduce cholesterol levels.

Ingredients:

2 tablespoons olive oil

1/2 cup diced onion

1 red bell pepper, diced

1 cup diced carrots

1 cup diced celery

2 cloves garlic, minced

2 cups broccoli florets

1 cup frozen edamame

1/2 teaspoon sea salt

1/4 teaspoon ground black pepper

2 cups cooked wholegrain rice

2 tablespoons low-sodium tamari

Preparation Time: 20 minutes

Method of Preparation:

1. Heat oil in a large skillet over medium heat.

2. Add onion, bell pepper, carrots, and celery and cook for about 5 minutes stirring frequently.

3. Add broccoli, edamame, salt, and pepper and stir-fry for 2 minutes.

4. Add cooked rice, tamari, and stir until combined.

5. Cook until heated through, about 5 minutes.

Serving Suggestions: Serve as a side dish or add your favorite protein for a complete meal.

Roasted Eggplant and Chickpea Salad

Packed with flavor and nutrition, it's perfect for those with cardiac disease, since its high fiber content helps control cholesterol levels and reduce inflammation.

Ingredients:

2 medium eggplants, cut into 1inch cubes

2 tablespoons olive oil

1/2 teaspoon sea salt

1/4 teaspoon ground black pepper

1 (15ounce) can chickpeas, drained and rinsed

1/2 cup diced red onion

1/2 cup diced cucumber

1/2 cup diced red bell pepper

1/2 cup diced cherry tomatoes

1/4 cup chopped fresh parsley

2 cloves garlic, minced

2 tablespoons freshly squeezed lemon juice

Preparation Time: 45 minutes

Method of Preparation:

1. Preheat oven to 425°F.

2. Toss eggplant cubes with olive oil, salt, and black pepper.

3.Spread on a parchment-lined baking sheet and roast for 25 minutes.

4. In a large bowl, mix together chickpeas, onion, cucumber, bell pepper, tomatoes, parsley, garlic, and lemon juice.

5. Add roasted eggplant and mix until combined.

Serving Suggestions: Serve as a light lunch or as a side dish.

Chickpea and Artichoke Stew

With several key nutrients, it's beneficial to those with cardiac disease since it can help to reduce cholesterol levels and support heart health.

Ingredients:

1 tablespoon olive oil

1 onion, diced

2 cloves garlic, minced

1 teaspoon ground cumin

1/2 teaspoon smoked paprika

1/4 teaspoon ground coriander

1/4 teaspoon cayenne pepper

1 (14.5ounce) can diced tomatoes

1 (15ounce) can chickpeas, drained and rinsed

1 (14ounce) can artichoke hearts, drained and rinsed

1 (14ounce) can low sodium vegetable broth

1/4 cup chopped fresh parsley

2 tablespoons freshly squeezed lemon juice

Preparation Time: 30 minutes

Method of Preparation:

1. Heat oil in a large saucepan over medium heat.

2. Add onion and cook until softened, about 5 minutes.

3. Add garlic, cumin, smoked paprika, coriander, and cayenne pepper and cook for 1 minute more.

4. Add diced tomatoes, chickpeas, artichokes, and vegetable broth and stir.

5. Bring stew to a boil over high heat, then reduce heat to low and simmer for 15 minutes.

6. Add parsley and lemon juice and simmer for an additional 5 minutes.

Serving Suggestions: Serve with your favorite whole grain and a side of steamed vegetables.

Roasted Portobello Mushroom Tacos

High in dietary fiber, it's a great option for those with cardiac disease, helping to reduce cholesterol and promote overall heart health.

Ingredients:

4 large portobello mushrooms

2 tablespoons olive oil

2 teaspoons freshly ground chili powder

1 teaspoon paprika

1/2 teaspoon sea salt

8 whole grain or corn taco shells

1/2 cup shredded red cabbage

1/4 cup diced red onion

1/4 cup diced tomato

1/4 cup sliced black olives

1/4 cup vegan sour cream

1/4 cup freshly squeezed lime juice

Preparation Time: 30 minutes

Method of Preparation:

1. Preheat oven to 375°F.

2. Brush mushrooms on both sides with olive oil and sprinkle chili powder, paprika, and salt.

3. Place mushrooms on a parchment lined baking sheet and bake for 20 minutes.

4. Once mushrooms are finished baking, slice into thin strips.

5. Place mushroom strips into taco shells and top with cabbage, onion, tomato, and olives.

6. Drizzle with sour cream and lime juice.

Serving Suggestions: Serve with your favorite salsa and a wedge of lime.

Greek Lentil Soup

An excellent source of protein, folate, and fiber, it can help reduce cholesterol levels and reduce inflammation, making it a heart-healthy meal.

Ingredients:

2 tablespoons olive oil

1 onion, diced

1 red bell pepper, diced

2 cloves garlic, minced

1 teaspoon ground cumin

1 teaspoon ground coriander

1/2 teaspoon dried oregano

1/4 teaspoon red pepper flakes

8 cups low-sodium vegetable broth

1 (15ounce) can fire-roasted diced tomatoes

1 (15ounce) can chickpeas, drained and rinsed

2 cups cooked green lentils

1/2 cup uncooked quinoa

3 tablespoons freshly squeezed lemon juice

1/4 cup chopped fresh parsley

Preparation Time: 35 minutes

Method of Preparation:

1. Heat oil in a large pot over medium heat.

2. Add onion, bell pepper, garlic, cumin, coriander, oregano and red pepper flakes and cook for 5 minutes.

3. Add vegetable broth, diced tomatoes, chickpeas, and lentils and bring the soup to a simmer.

4. Reduce heat to low and simmer for 15 minutes.

5. Add quinoa, lemon juice, and parsley and simmer for an additional 10 minutes.

Serving Suggestions: Serve with a side of crusty wholegrain bread.

CONCLUSION

In conclusion, this book has provided you with essential recipes to help you get started with a Plant-based cardiac diet.

With this knowledge, you can start making small changes to your diet to improve your overall health and well being.

Additionally, you can work with the nutritionist to identify and design an eating pattern that is best for you.

Although the transition from a traditional diet to a Plant-based one can be difficult, it is possible.

With determination, dedication, and delicious recipes from this cookbook, you can become an expert in Plant-based nutrition and take charge of your heart health.

Made in the USA
Monee, IL
27 December 2023

50532188R00039